Praise for TRICKS OF LIGHT

The poems in Thaddeus Rutkowski's newest volume, *Tricks of Light*, are plainsongs: They don't aim for transcendence (although transcendent moments are achieved with a genius's nonchalance) but remain steadily in the world as it is. For Rutkowski, the world's too often a terrifying and unforgiving place. But Rutkowski also knows that this is the place—the only place—where transformation is possible. And so these plainsongs remind me of a walk a sage might take along an ordinary stone path—the occasional shiny object underfoot only serving to acknowledge a wisdom already possessed. I would walk with Rutkowski anywhere.

—JANET KAPLAN, author of *Ecotones*

Tricks of Light inhabits that liminal space between what we see and what we think we see, what we know and what perpetually eludes us. Artfully wry and delightfully awry, these are poems rooted in keen observation of a life as it unfolds. They explore community and isolation, likeness and difference, country ways and city ways, duty and desire. Rutkowski's introspective voice measures the self against the strange and ever-changing world, a place where children leave home and strangers rest unexpectedly on doorsteps. Rutkowski approaches his subjects with uncompromising drollery. "Always" reasons Rutkowski, "is definitely not forever." We get close calls, flat tires, slow fixes, listless turtles, temple-enshrined teeth, frozen roses, and one tough mango. Yet these poems resound with earnestness, affirming that to persevere through life's acute absurdities is not merely decent, but uncommonly noble. Come to *Tricks of Light* expecting deft poetics; leave steeped in luminosity.

—JOSEPH J. CAPISTA, author of *Intrusive Beauty*

For Randi Hoffman and Shay Rutkowski

Contents

TRICKS OF LIGHT

great weather for MEDIA
New York City

JUST ONE WORD

I wrote one word today.
I changed the word "the" to "my"
in the phrase "Through the window."

I thought "my" might be more specific,
might let you know the window
belonged to me. And the whole text,
other than that word, was about me,
about my state of mind.

But maybe changing that one word
wasn't really writing. Maybe it was editing,
and I should have said, "I edited one word today."
And maybe I should have received credit for that,
because editing one word is more than editing no words.

Beyond that, it is editing *my* word,
not someone else's word,
and so I helped myself, in a way.

LIGHTS IN DARKNESS

You might think you're seeing shooting stars
in the purple, not-yet-black sky:
points of light over a cornfield
and over the tops of trees—
shooting stars like the ones you'd see
when you go to the cemetery,
where there is no human light
and the sky is pitch-black.
But you would be wrong.

What you're seeing are the flash trails
of fireflies that have flown high
and appear to be in the stratosphere,
blinking their code to other fireflies,
so that those closer to the ground
can separate the inviting flashes
from the uninteresting ones,
and can fly to the thin air above the earth,
to join their partners.

WHERE I'M FROM

I don't think anyone outside of a ten-mile radius
has heard of where I'm from.
The one-street town lies downstream
from another one-street town.

I never made it more than a mile or two from my home.
For transportation, I used a bike, my feet, or skates.
Surrounded by nature, I had no choice but to appreciate it.

I was raised as white, but I'm not white.
My father saw no difference between races,
while my mother never forgot hers.

My goal was to learn to drive,
then climb into a car with a full tank of gas,
floor the accelerator, and blow out of there.

FARMERS AND DOVE

When sunlight hits the higher points
and the lower places remain in shadow,
two farmers harvest corn together.
One drives a pickup truck,
while the other follows alongside,
stripping ears off stalks
and tossing them into the truck bed.

On a telephone wire above the farmers,
a mourning dove coos for what's lost,
for some unspecified thing that's missing
The calls aren't sad for the dove,
only for those who are listening.
For those of us who know what's missing,
the sounds of the bird remind us of what's lost.

CLAW MARKS

The trunk of this beech tree
is scored with dents just far enough apart

to indicate fingernails, or an animal's nails,
or the claws of a bear, hungry for beechnuts.

The small, oily nuts, covered in burrs,
will help sustain a bear through winter.

The nuts are high up in the tree,
but a bear is a good climber,

with claws that can pierce the bark
on a smooth, iron-like trunk.

The bear is long gone. It's winter now,
too cold for bears and other hibernators.

The bear's marks remain in the bark,
at just the right distance to mark its reach.

BEING ALONE

When I'm alone with myself,
I am not where I want to be.
There is just me.
There aren't two of us,
It is not me and my shadow, cavorting.
There's only one,
and that's not enough to keep me company.
Sometimes, I don't want myself around.
I want myself to go away,
but I can't tell myself to do that.

VIEW FROM A BRIDGE

Looking down from a bridge
I see a large boat being pushed
by a small boat hitched to its side.
The two are fighting the current,
barely making headway,
if they are getting anywhere at all.

I'm pedaling toward the apex of the bridge
in the lowest gear my bicycle has.
For a moment, I look over the railing
to understand the motion of barge and tugboat.
Soon my path will switch from uphill
to down, and I will be flying.

DROPS IN A BUCKET

Holding a pail, a boy stares at the water
running in a gutter next to the street.
He's looking with interest,
as if he might do something with this water,
this overflow from a fire hydrant.
He might catch some of it
and take it somewhere. But where?
Maybe to another gutter, a dry one
that needs water, but his small bucket
won't do much to fill that other water course.
He would have to make many trips
back and forth, from running water
to dry course, and his effort would only serve
to satisfy his own curiosity
about what he could do with a pail
and an endless supply of water.

THE SPECK

It's just a speck on the ocean,
a dark dot in gray water,
so far away it might be a trick of light—
a shadow, not an object—
but I think it is an actual thing.

I want the speck to be alive,
to be the back of a seal or a dolphin.
But the shape doesn't move,
though it bobs in the water,
like a bird, brooding,
letting the waves carry it,

I'm not going to find out
what the thing is.
My vision is limited, filtered by glass,
shielded from the weather.
I am too comfortable here,
in this climate-controlled building.

HORSE SENSE

Why would someone keep a statue
of a horse in the yard?
I could understand having a statue of a deer
as a reminder that real deer live nearby.
The statue won't run away.
But a real horse won't run away, either,
unless it is spooked,
and we won't spook it,
because it could be our friend,
if we treat it in a friendly manner.
A real horse could be so friendly
that it might become our best friend
and replace the dog in our world.

WEED GARDENER

She grows weed—not weeds—in her garden.
She doesn't plant seeds,
because seeds will grow into plants with seeds.
She buys a small female plant
from a cannabis store
and lets it grow until it is several feet tall,
and is filled with flowers and pollen,
but no seeds.

COLD DAYS IN FLORIDA

When the temperature drops to forty degrees,
people don't want to walk around.
It is too cold to be outside.
They stay inside and wait
until the days get warmer.

The temperature rarely drops below forty.
But once it dropped to twenty-eight.
When that happened, birds started to die.
All around the bay, all kinds of birds
keeled over, because of the cold.
Along with the birds, people started to die,
but not everyone succumbed to the cold.
Only old people died;
they couldn't take the shock
of a cold snap in Florida.

STEAMROLLED

I come to where I usually take a detour—
a stretch where the pavement has been roughed up
in preparation for new pavement.
Now, I see machines laying new blacktop,
so I ride on the new surface.
The material is sticky, almost soft, maybe warm,
and I wonder if my bike's tires are sinking in.
Presently, I hear people yelling, "Sidewalk!"
I know they mean I should get off the street,
but I don't get off.
Then I hear a horn that comes from a steamroller.
I ride around the monster machine
to where the new blacktop ends.
The road is rough, gouged,
so I ride onto the sidewalk.
I didn't know steamrollers had horns.

PENNIES

If I see a penny on the street,
I won't pick it up.
But if I drop a penny,
I will pick it up.
I have plans for that penny.
I know how many pennies
I have in my pocket
how many I'll have to use
to get back a nickel or a dime
when I receive change.
I don't hoard pennies.
It's too much work.
I want to spend them
(they're worth a cent each),
get rid of them by using them.
I don't want to throw them away
or scatter them on the ground.
If I did that, who would want them?

SIX CENTS

I see six pennies on the street.
Six seems a lot, so I pick them up.

I already have three pennies in my pocket
and think I can buy a ten-cent piece of candy.
But the store clerk won't spot me a penny.
I have to beg the manager for a one-cent credit.
He gives it to me, and two weeks later,
I pay back the loan.

The clerk doesn't know what to do
with the extra penny.
He has probably forgotten
it was for that ten-cent piece of candy.

When I go back two weeks later,
the penny is still there,
on the arm of the cash register,
where the clerk left it.

SLACKING OFF

I'm not happy
that I'm not doing my own work.
I'm not doing it today,
and I wasn't doing it yesterday.
I'm breaking my pattern of doing work,
even if only a little work, every day.
I want to put down
a few lines, a few words
that didn't exist before.
If my oeuvre were a tree,
I'd want to add a shoot, a leaf or a twig each day.

But I understand
there is more important work to be done:
work for other people
who are in a hurry, who need me
to help them with their work.
So that's what I'm doing—helping them—
hoping I'll get back to my own work tomorrow.

OWNING MY SPEECH

Can I own the way I talk?
Can I possess it, like an object,
and let the person I'm talking to
know that I own it?

I don't want someone else
to own my speech.
I don't want to acquiesce
to someone else's interpretation.

So I'll say things loud and clear,
and, if I have to,
I'll shout things in your ear,
so we'll both know what I mean.

CLOSE CALL

I'm sworn at, again,
While riding my bicycle,
this time by a white-haired woman.
"We've got the light, asshole," she calls.
I have to admit that
I didn't notice a traffic light at all,
let alone which color was lit
(we're not at an intersection;
we're at a bend in the bike path).
But I do know this:
I came too close for this woman's comfort,
and she felt compelled to use profanity
to let me know I did something wrong.
Honestly, I don't see it that way.
She was in my lane; I wasn't in hers.
She should look both ways before crossing,
and if she needs to jump out of the way,
then she should jump quietly.

FOREIGN FILLINGS

I'm asked if the fillings in my teeth
were done in a different country.
I wonder if foreign fillings look different,
if they are higher or lower on the tooth,
or have a different color.
Maybe what looks different is my face,
as if I'm from a different country
and had my earlier dental work done there.

"What country do you mean?"
I ask the dentist and his assistant
because I can't quite figure out
what country they think I'm from.
Maybe they don't know;
maybe all they know is,
I don't look like they do.
I wait for their answer with my mouth open.

MYSTERY BIRD

As I roll along a side street on my bike,
I see what looks like a large bird,
standing on the pavement with its wings spread
at a span of five or six feet.
This bird could be a raptor ready for takeoff.

I roll closer and see that the wings
are actually the legs of a warning sign
face down on the street,
having been kicked over by a drunk person,
or knocked over by a swerving car.
It is the kind of sign that would say,
"WORK AREA" on its orange-painted face
if it were standing upright,
but it has been toppled next to a crater
in the middle of my path.

ANOTHER FLAT

I sense a telltale rumble as I ride my bike.
I stop and squeeze the back tire
and feel it is soft.
After I roll another block, it is dead flat.
I have a couple more miles to go
and no choice but to walk.
But I know this route
and know of a bike-repair shop.
I head for it as quickly as I can.
Sweat gathers on my back and seeps into my backpack.
I didn't know I could generate so much sweat
just by walking on a hot day.

A half-hour later, I arrive at Excelsior Bike Repair,
but it is closed.
I don't know why it would be closed
on a Thursday afternoon.
Maybe it has gone out of business,
because no one except for me
ever gets a flat tire in these parts.

NO FIX

Why go for the quick fix?
Why not go for the slow fix?
Both questions assume
there is a problem and a fix.
The only difference is how long
the fix will take.

I admit there is a problem,
but I'm not sure there is a fix
There are some problems
that cannot be solved
in any amount of time,
no matter how one tries to fix them.

SOFT PROJECTILE

While riding on my bicycle,
I feel something hit the side of my head.
It is soft, like a bird or a pillow,
and it makes no sound—no cracking
of a hard object making contact with my skull.

I'm riding the wrong way, I know it.
An approaching rider could have hit me
with his sleeve, just to correct me.
I look back at two riders who have passed.
Neither one is looking at me and swearing.

I look to see if a pigeon might have hit me.
No bird is on the ground;
no harm was done to any bird.
It wasn't a bird that hit me.

I might have been hit
by a chamois cloth, a sponge, or a mop head
thrown by a car driver annoyed with me.

HIT AGAIN

I drift to the left to avoid a biker
coming the wrong way, toward me,
and a car hits me with its side door.
It is a yellow cab that was speeding past
as I drifted toward it.

I hear and feel the impact against my arm,
and I think, "Not again."
It is the second time
I've been hit in a couple of weeks;
the first was on my other arm.
But I can use the arm that was hit now.
I can lift it and move it. I feel nothing
beyond a dull pain in the elbow.

I see the cab has stopped.
Maybe the driver heard the impact, too,
and wants to see if I'm all right,
or maybe he has stopped for a traffic light.

TURTLE'S COLD DAY

Outside, the temperature is below freezing,
while inside, our turtle isn't eating; she's listless.
Maybe she is stuck between hibernating
and living an active turtle's life.
She spends a lot of time underwater, sleeping,
and very little time on her shelf, basking.

The sun doesn't hit directly at this time of year.
To catch some rays, she has to pull herself up
to a corner of her aquarium and extend her neck.
She can stay that way for a long while,
head in the sun. She's a strong turtle.
But she is not bathing her nose in sunlight now.

When I don't see her, I worry.
I know she can hold her breath for hours.
I don't want to wait that long for her to appear,
so I tap on her basking shelf, and she stirs,
pokes her head out of the water,
torn between fear and the prospect of food.

HEAD SCRATCHING

I know why our turtle stretches her legs—
she does it to cool off.
She can regulate her body temperature
through the skin of her legs
(she can't control her blood temperature;
she's as cold or hot as the air around her).

But I don't understand
why she scratches her head,
why she brings up one foreleg
and strokes from her eye to her nose.
Is something there, a mosquito?
(I see no mites, ticks or other pests.)
Or is she trying to figure out
the answers to difficult questions,
such as where she came from,
why she is here, and where she is going?
Those questions, for a turtle, are hard to answer,
just as they are hard for humans to answer.
In fact, I'd say that any person who has the answers
doesn't really know what he or she is talking about.
That person is no smarter than a turtle scratching its head.

BRIEF LIFE

Our turtle has laid three eggs
on the floor, next to a small ledge
on which she balances. It is as if
she has put the eggs below the ground,
where they will be protected.
She makes digging, scooping motions
with her hind legs, as if she is
covering the eggs with soil or sand.
She isn't done yet.
Her body shakes in a labor
that lasts an hour or more,
as she produces two more eggs.

Her concern is laying eggs.
My concern, however, is that she
doesn't crush and eat the eggs,
and make a mess of the yolk and white,
to be discovered and cleaned up.
So I pick her eggs up off the floor
and dispose of them.
Soon, I notice she is looking
for the missing eggs. She knows
they were hers and now they are gone.

NOTHING IN COMMON

I used to think I'd have something in common
with people of color, anyone of color
of any age, and of any color.
It didn't matter, because we'd had
the same experience,
were looked at the same way
by the people around us,
by everyone who had the unvoiced thought:
"He (or she) is not like me!"
People who'd been the target
would be friends with me.

But I was wrong.
Factors other than color
were more important to people of color
when it came to being friends with me.
I didn't know what was on their minds.
They must have seen a likeness,
but they also saw a difference
that we could not get past.
They might have been thinking:
"He looks different, but what is he?"

ANGRY MAN

A man gets angry with me
for leaving work early,
so I explain I'm going to another job,
but he doesn't accept that excuse,
so I tell him I'll quit the other job,
even though I'm supposed to be there
when I make the call to quit.
The man is happy now;
he thinks I can work another couple of hours.
Then I realize I have to teach a class,
I can't work any job on this day,
and I'll have to make the man angry again.

GETTING THE BEST OF ME

I don't know what to do with my anger.
Should I walk away from the person
who is making me angry?
Or should I say something
right to that person's face?
If I walk away, I will avoid a fight.
If I say something, I will start a fight.
and two people will be angry.
Two is worse than one.

It would be better—ideal—
if I never encountered a riling situation.
But who is able to live that way?
Who follows the middle path?
Buddhist high priests? The Buddha himself?
I am not like they are.
I let anger get the best of me every day.

THE FEAR, REVISITED

The fear hits again,
as my body changes to defend itself
against an unknown attacker.
It is no longer a feeling
in the pit of my stomach.
It is more like a gut reaction,
a soreness, a tenderness, a vulnerability,
and I am reluctant to do anything,
to venture into the unknown,
because that can bring on more fear.
But I'll do it. I'll go out and see people
(the most frightening activity in the world)
and hope the fear corrects itself.

WAXED PAPER MUSEUM

For Sparrow

I don't want to go to the Wax Museum.
I want to go to a Waxed Paper Museum,
where varieties of waxed paper through the ages
are displayed in vitrines and frames,
and where the gift shop
sells objects wrapped in paraffin-coated paper.

In the museum, we won't have to worry
about whether the wax statues
accurately portray the people they stand for
or even whether the people cast in wax
belong in a museum.
We will just appreciate the craft
of making paper that keeps moisture out
and freshness in, for days.

CAPPUCCINO FAUX PAS

In Italy, I was called a baby
by a wait staffer
because I asked for a cappuccino
in the evening, after a meal.
I didn't know that cappuccino
is usually served in the morning,
before any food.
"One cappuccino for the *bebè*,"
the woman said in Italian,
and I got the cup I asked for.
I would have changed my order,
but didn't know how to, in Italian.
So I just bore the humiliation
of sipping cappuccino like a baby.

NO PARKING

Found poem, Hong Kong

Vehicle waiting
will be prosecuted
without warning.

IN THE BUDDHA'S TOOTH TEMPLE

We walk into a temple to see the relic:
a tooth of the Buddha found in Myanmar,
long after the Buddha was alive.

We stop at a series of altars,
one for each sign of the zodiac.
In each section are a hundred tiny Buddhas,
each with a unique hand gesture or facial expression,
like those of the soldiers in China's old capital,
whose terra-cotta bodies are identical,
but whose faces are individual.

We proceed upstairs, as all around us
the chants of monks
come through an amplified system
and fill the temple.

We pass a giant prayer wheel
and reach the room with the relic.
(I wonder if it is a molar or an incisor.)

No one is in the room.
There is no crowd around the pedestal
holding the tooth of the prince
who gave up everything he had
to gain everything he needed.

FOUNTAIN LIGHTS

I can see a circular fountain, dry now,
with bright lights mounted in its middle.
It could be a movie set,
but how would a dry, well-lit fountain
fit into a movie?
Would children run around the fountain,
playing some kind of chase game?
Perhaps the movie lights
have nothing to do with the fountain.
They could be aimed at vendors' stands.
The fountain, shut down for the winter,
is just a convenient place
to attach lights this holiday season.

THE HOLIDAYS

I remember the times I was alone on the holidays,
when I looked for something exciting to do
but couldn't find anything that excited me
because I was alone.
I walked along the streets,
looking for something I couldn't find.
I did not celebrate; I did nothing special.
I felt I had no choice.
That's why I don't get too excited
about the holidays now.

FRUIT OF STEEL

When I try to peel its skin with a knife,
when I swear at it and it remains unmoved,
when I slice the flesh from the seed
    and fail to separate the flesh,
when I serve it on a plate
    and the pieces slide off the plate,
when I pick up a piece and bite into it
    and the fruit tastes hard and raw,
I can tell this is one tough mango.

DRIFTING APART

When people ask me to get together,
      it usually takes me months to make a date.
I will put off the meeting until I reach the limit
      of friendship.
If I wait any longer, we won't meet at all.
We will just have memories of our last meeting,
      and of things we said to each other then.
Our impressions of who we are will be frozen
      in that moment
And if we ever do see each other again,
      we will be shocked by how much we've changed
      over the years,
and we will wonder what happened to the person
      we knew back then.

NO FRIENDS

I don't know if I have close friends,
the kind of people I'd call on the phone
when I have a big issue to discuss.
Maybe I don't have issues I'd consider big,
and that's why I don't want to speak to anyone.

However, if a close relative dies,
I would call a couple of people,
more out of obligation
than a desire for any comfort I might receive.
I suppose this means
I am living "inside myself,"
disconnected from others and the world.

My new task could be to call one friend per day,
whether or not I have anything to say.
This might become a healthy pattern.
No doubt we would find something to talk about.

GLASS AND TEARS

He was watching some television—
Christmas songs on a DVD—
and getting ready for bed,
when he dropped a glass.
It was a new glass; he wasn't attached to it.
But when it gave up its life,
he started to cry, not just for the glass,
but for everything else that was broken.

Those broken things came rushing at him
as he swept up the fragments,
knowing he would not spot them all.
He would find slivers of glass later,
when he stepped on them with bare feet.

UNIDENTIFIED STATIONARY OBJECT

I see an object on the basement floor
in the light from the airshaft.
The oblong, motionless thing
looks like a dead mouse;
its gray-and-black pattern
fits the wild species.

I wonder if I should complain
or just pick up the carcass and trash it.
But when I get closer,
I see the "mouse" is a pigeon feather,
a long one from a wing,
a feather the size of a house mouse,
beautiful in its way,
now missing from its owner.

Maybe the bird was fighting
with a rival over a potential mate,
or maybe it hit the side of the building
while gliding down the airshaft.
Or maybe birds' feathers fall out spontaneously,
like strands of hair from human heads.

THE COLLECTOR

A bottle collector
is sitting on our doorstep,
sorting through a large bag,
removing the caps from plastic containers
and throwing the capless containers
into another large bag.

She's wearing a head scarf,
and she doesn't seem to have an age.
But when I walk around her,
I see she is quite old.
She must have gotten in
because the door is open
and she knows where to find the recyclables.

I leave the block and come back,
and see her again,
on a different stoop,
without her head scarf
and I see she is so old
her hair is thin on top.
She must be waiting
for another door to open
so she can get the discards.

DOWN IN THE DUMPSTER

Most of the dumpsters I've visited
have contained debris from demolition:
Sheetrock, studs, corner beading, plaster dust,
garbage bags filled with mystery material
(I haven't cared to discover what was hidden inside.)

Once, however, my wife came in
with a perfectly good object from a dumpster:
a scented candle from our next-door flower shop.
"You should go down and look," she said.
"Lots of these candles were thrown away."

I went down and found large candles, plain tapers,
and candles to be burned in glass holders.
There were dozens, maybe hundreds, of them.
Later, I saw a destitute man sitting in a local park,
burning a large candle and selling the rest.

COFFEE SHOP ENCOUNTER

A woman approaches me and asks,
"Would you mind getting me a chocolate muffin?"
At first, she looks young, with her thick blond hair,
but her red face makes her look older.
I hesitate, and another man gives her a couple of dollars.
"I only needed fifty cents," she says.

She buys a muffin and sits next to me.
A moment later she says something.
I ask, "What was that?"
She says, "I was talking to the panels up there,"
and I see there are painted areas on the ceiling.

"I'm not from Blue Ridge," she says.
"Where are you from?" I ask.
"From here," she says, "New York.
I don't remember where in the city.

"I can't eat chocolate," she adds,
"but it's the only kind of muffin worth eating."

I give her a little money.
As she gets up to leave, she says,
"I have to get shampoo and conditioner."

NOISE TO MY EARS

I often give money to street musicians,
because I admire their talent
and their sounds make me happier than I had been.

But I don't give to people who only pretend
to play their instruments.
If I am walking through a passage
between two subway stations,
trapped, with no immediate way out,
and several "musicians"
are blowing randomly into horns,
or pounding desperately on drums,
I will not be impressed enough
or made happy enough
to reach into my pocket for a handout.
My ear is not trained, but I can tell
when what I'm hearing is unpleasant.

IN THE MEDIAN

While I wait to cross the street,
I see a bird the size of a sparrow,
but it is not a sparrow. It is not brown and white.
It is olive green on top and yellow green on its breast.
There was a time when I might have known
what kind of bird this is,
but now it is like none I've ever seen.

It hops over dark-green leaves in the tall blades
that have collapsed in the cold.
The roses are frozen but still identifiable as roses.
The bird goes from place to place,
aiming with its beak for crumbs or seeds
among the pieces of trash that people throw
while they wait in the median to cross the street.

SEAL SOUNDS

I wonder if these early-morning cries
have come across the water
and echoed off a building,
so I walk to an open alley
and look out at the dark ocean,
but the noises don't come again.

Later, I hear what I think
might be the barking of a seal.
It is not a dog; it is too melodious.
But there are no seals here;
I have never seen a seal in the Atlantic.

My question is moot.
The sound I hear is coming from a swing set.
A child is swinging. The swing chain
is rubbing against its metal anchor.

SHADOW BICYCLE

Out of the corner of my eye
I see a bicycle cut through traffic behind me,
the same way I am cutting through traffic
But it is matte black, the shadow of a bicycle,
and when I look back I don't see it at all.
Was it the shadow of my own bicycle?
Or was it a ghost bicycle and rider
following me as a warning
that I could become a ghost biker
if I'm not careful as I cut through traffic?

HOLDING THE CHICKEN

The farmer says we can hold a chicken.
He says they look big, but we'll realize
they are mostly feathers.

When I hold the bird,
I pin its wings, as instructed,
but I squeeze too tightly,
as if I'm holding a football,
and the bird squawks.
It opens its beak as if it might peck,
so I turn its head away from my face.

When I hand the bird to my wife,
she holds it against her chest
as if she is holding a baby,
and the bird becomes calm.
It doesn't squawk or flap its wings
or try to peck at anyone's face.

COMPULSION

Before I leave our apartment,
I check the door in patterns of threes and sevens.
I turn the knob to the right three times
and push the door three times with my hand.
Then I turn the knob three times,
then once, then three times
and hit the door seven times with my palm.

If my small daughter is with me,
she might ask, "Are you afraid of someone breaking in?"
And I might say, "Yes,"
though that would not begin to express my fear.
I would try to test the lock again,
but she would say, "That's enough. Let's go,"
and I would have to stop.

IN THE VALLEY

In the Amish store,
white-capped women greet us.
One lights a kerosene lamp
to illuminate the herbs for sale.
When one speaks,
we hear her Pennsylvania Dutch accent.
In their long dresses, they study us
as we make our small purchase.

My daughter and I walk out of the store
and look across the valley,
toward the hill of unleafed trees below a rainy sky.
A pickup truck skims by.
"Culture shock," my daughter says.
She means the landscape,
but she could mean the highway and the vehicle,
if she were speaking for the Amish.

READING IN BED

I say I'm going to read in bed,
and she asks, "Can I read with you?"
"Sure," I say, but before she gets there
I pull up a blanket to cover my body.
She easily climbs the ladder
and crawls over me.

"We could read *The Lord of the Rings* aloud," I say,
remembering that, years before,
I read the book to her
but didn't get past the first chapter,
about Bilbo's birthday party,
where he puts on the Ring and vanishes.

I show her the book I'm reading, called *Grendel*,
and tell her it's hard to read.
She says she read it freshman year in high school .
"How were you able to do that?" I ask.
"It was different from the other books
we had to read," she says.

I ask what book she's reading.
I see flames on the front cover.
The title is *How to Set a Fire*,
and the book is about a teenage arson club.
"It's young adult but sold in the adult section," she says.

"I'm going to sleep," I say.
and she starts to crawl over me
in the opposite direction.
I move over so she can get past more easily.

COLOR COORDINATION

Our daughter cares
about the colors of her clothes.

When she chooses a new hat,
she picks a light-brown one,
the color of maple wood.
I point out that it matches
the color of her hair.

She likes the colors I'm wearing:
a maroon shirt over a dark-green tee.
She says those colors go well together.
She also notices my new sneakers:
black with white stripes.
"Those are good ones," she says.

But her coat, she says, is not her.
I don't know why it's not her.
It looks warm, with a faux-fur collar,
and comes past her knees.
I should ask, if I really want to know.
But I am not quick enough to find out.

EMPTY NEST

I have a feeling that something is missing,
because our child is no longer living with us.
I was focused on her, and on her only,
and now I'm not focused on her
unless she contacts me,
and she doesn't contact me often.
I could contact her,
but I would need a good reason.
She and I aren't in the habit of waving
at each other over distance, in cyberspace,
just for the sake of waving.

I can see this emptiness as freedom,
a space in which to do what I like,
I don't need to fill the space
with someone else to take care of,
someone like a pet: a dog or a cat.
I don't need a pet to feed
and/or walk on a regular basis.
I don't need to worry about the pet's survival
when I go away from home for a while.
A pet wouldn't make me happier,
though I would make a pet happier.

MOON AND AIRPLANE

Before dawn, a star sits in front
of the half moon, and nothing else
is close to the two objects in the sky.
After sunrise, the moon is still visible,
but the star has vanished;
in its place is a jet contrail.

I'm on the ground, looking up.
Our plane is at the gate.
It's not the kind of plane
that has been grounded as unsafe,
but it's close:
an early-generation Boeing 737.
Soon, we will cross the path of the moon.

MIMICRY

I'm looking for wildlife next to the water
when I see a snail on a bench.
This bench would be a good place for a snail.
It is cool and damp: the perfect surface
for a snail to slide on.

But on closer inspection,
the "snail" turns out to be a wad of gum.
The lump is the right color and shape
for a snail: gray and round.
It is also the perfect color and shape
for a wad of gum.

YELLOW-GREEN HILLS OF PENNSYLVANIA

The mountains—the hills, really—
are yellow-green, in transition
from bare trees to leafed trees.
I don't know how long this color will last.
If I were fishing now,
I could walk to the water and cast my line
without getting it tangled in leaves.
If I want to see something distant, a house, say,
I can see it through the trees.
These yellow-green constellations
are only buds, and when the sun hits,
the whole mountain lights up.
That is, assuming the mountain—a hill, really—
is not covered by fog.

DREAM DECODED

I'm given a book by a young poet,
but I've already bought the book,
so when the poet gives me a copy,
I have two copies for the price of one.

I could have had one copy for free
and no second copy.
That would have been more economical
and it would have been all I needed.

But in the scheme of things,
the difference between buying a book
and being given one isn't significant.
I'll hold on to both copies.

SHE HAS SOME COPIES

I have none of my own books with me.
But I might need them.
I might need to see what I've written,
so I can share it with others.
But I have no way of getting my books.
I'm in a city hundreds of miles
from where I live.
I have many copies there, but none here.

I see a solution to the problem:
I can ask my host,
the woman in whose house I'm staying,
if I can borrow my books from her shelf.
I think she has some copies,
but I don't know where she keeps them.
I just know they are here somewhere,
spines out, on a shelf.

CLASS COUP

The U.S. president takes over a class I'm teaching.
He hasn't been there all semester,
but he shows up for the final exam.
He will score the test and give final grades.

I'm concerned that he doesn't know
enough about the students' work
to assign final grades,
but I understand he won't be stopped.

I ask for his email address,
because I think we should talk about grading,
but a security officer tells me it's not possible.
I have no clearance to email the president.

Another official collects the exam booklets
and puts them on the floor of the president's limousine.
"Wait," I say, but nothing further is needed from me.
The students will receive grades they didn't expect.

WORTH NOTHING, BUT WORTH SELLING

My mother has sold some of my clothes.
I remember a couple of the items:
a black T-Shirt with a Metallica theme,
a green button-down shirt of the Polo/Lauren variety.
I don't know how she got hold of these things.
But they are gone, and I'll miss them.
I don't begrudge my mother
any money she got for the clothes,
because she has so many things
that are worth nothing.

WHERE IS HE?

A young man calls for his friend
as he goes from door to door
in the library basement.
He calls at one locked restroom,
then the other,
but there is no answer.
He knocks on the elevator door and calls out.
"I can't find my friend," he says to no one,
and a librarian answers: "You can't go in there."
She means he can't go into a closed room.
"I'm looking for my friend," he says.

I believe his friend is real,
and his friend is really lost.
But I don't know if the friend
considers himself a friend.
If he did, he wouldn't leave the library
without saying anything.

MAN FISHING

At the railing next to the river,
a man pulls his line in from the choppy, brown water.
There is drag on the line,
and I think he might be reeling in a fish,
though I've never seen anyone
catch a fish here before.

Sometimes the man cranks the reel;
other times he grabs the line
with his hand and pulls,
but he doesn't seem to be making progress.
I watch for a few minutes,
waiting to see what's on the line,
but the end of the line,
where there might be a fish or a crab,
never appears.

BOY PEEING

I have to walk my bike
around a boy and his mother.
The boy is peeing next to a small tree,
but not through his fly—
his pants are around his knees.
His mother is supporting him
with a hand on his shoulder.
Other people are walking around them.
I park my bike and look back
as the two walk away.

I'm thinking, if it were me, having to pee,
I'd have crossed the street
and gone into the park on the other side.
I'd have looked for a public restroom
though I might not have favored it—
it might have been smelly.
Or I would have found a bush to hide behind.
But I don't know if I would have done this when I was two.
How would I have broken it to my mother
that I didn't want an audience while peeing?

IN THE VOIR DIRE ROOM

Well, I don't want to lie,
but I don't want to be here,
so I suggest gently that I might be biased
in favor of the claimant.
I always want to stick it to the big guy
and give back to the little guy.

But I might not succeed
in my request for dismissal.
In which case, I'll be annoyed
and will decide in favor of the claimant,
no matter what.

I don't care if the driver of a city bus
actually caused an injury to a pedestrian.
I'm going to drain the city
of as much money as possible,
because I don't want to be here, in this plain room,
waiting to be picked for a jury.

MY BROTHER'S PASSING

My brother died
on a stormy day in July,
He didn't kill himself,
as he had often threatened to do.
He started coughing blood and couldn't stop.
He went outside, then couldn't walk.
He didn't get past the concrete steps
that led to the yard.

My mother was with him through it;
she saw him fall away.
She called me, told me at about five p.m.
Her news was all I could think about,
even though I went to a party that night.
I wanted to tell everyone there what had happened,
But I didn't tell anyone. How could I?
I celebrated with everyone else.

THE VAPORS

While I'm standing in a bar,
holding my second mug of beer,
I stumble back a couple of steps,
and spill some of my drink.
I seem to be unable to speak or see.
But I don't drop the glass in my hand,
and I don't fall on the floor.
I "come to" after a couple of seconds.
The people around me ask,
"Are you all right?"
And I say yes, but I get off my feet,
sit on a stool, and grip the edge of the bar.
I don't want to alarm anyone
by lurching backward,
while my eyes roll upward.
I don't want to hear again
their statements of concern.

LOOKING MY AGE

My daughter says I look old,
older than I looked just two months ago—
the last time I saw her.
"Do you mean my eyes?" I ask.
"It's your whole face," she says.

I remember a time my father visited
his family—his wife and us children—
after he'd been away for a couple of months.
We were sitting around the dining table,
and my brother and sister and I
asked him, "When are you going to get old?"
We found the question hilarious
because he wasn't old yet.
We kept asking, so we could keep laughing.
We were three, four, and seven years old.
Our father was thirty-three.

ONE-TENTH

A Chinese philosopher said:
"Live to old age, study to old age.
There remain three-tenths that cannot be known."

I am on my way to old age, I am still studying,
and I don't know one-tenth of what can be known.

I inch ahead, adding, bit by bit, to what I know.
But as I add, other things slip away.
I hope I add more than I lose.

Who knows? Maybe the sand in the hourglass
is running out faster than I'm replenishing it.
There isn't much I can do about that,
except to turn the hourglass over.

SHE HAS A MAP OF THE CITY

When my daughter asks me to sit next to her,
I think she isn't serious,
because if it were the other way around,
if I were to ask her to sit next to me,
I would expect her to say no.
But now she says, "You have to look at my screen,"
and so I come to look at her computer.

She has a map of the city on the screen.
She can trace street routes with a red line.
She finds the distance I ride my bicycle
to get to school: five miles one way.
She draws the path she runs from home,
down around the tip of Manhattan,
and back up the other side: seven miles round trip.

She shows me where she ran a half-marathon
twice around a portion of Central Park.
I remember that day: Her mother and I
met her at the end of the run,
as an announcer called her name.
She was neither first nor last,
but she covered the thirteen miles.

PERSONAL SPACE

When my daughter asks for a hug, I'm surprised,
because she doesn't usually want a hug.
She is protective of her personal space.
So I quickly say, "Yes," and wrap my arms
around her bare shoulders.
Her body is light, not like mine.
I don't quite get my arms all the way around.
I hesitate to do that, to encircle her completely,
but I squeeze my hands against her shoulder blades
and say, "Bear hug!" as I pull her toward me.
If I'm going to hug, I want it to be strong.
She doesn't really hug me back.
She just accepts my hug.

VACATION ANXIETY

I don't know why I'm anxious
while on vacation with my family.
I don't know if I have good reason to panic,
or if the cause is in my mind.

I do know the anxiety is real.
I feel it most of the time,
while walking along the street,
studying the sprays of flowers,
finding a place in the shifting sand,
testing the water with my skin,
bobbing on waves or diving through surf.

Invented or not,
the fear doesn't leave me
for more than the short times
during which I can't avoid enjoying myself.

WHEN WILL I GET SOMETHING TO GIVE?

At some point,
if you are going in the right direction,
you will have more to give.
What would that be,
that which you have more of?
More compassion? More sympathy? More money?
Many people would like compassion and sympathy,
but still more would like money.
I feel in my bones this is true.
But my mind tells me it is wrong.
Greed for money is a manifestation of taking.
Giving money is OK, though.
I wish I had more of it to give.
But in order to have it,
I would have to be given it
by someone, or by more than one person.
The question is, when will I get it?

GOD WILL SEE

"Are you in a hurry?" a young Hasidic man asks
as I wait on my bicycle at an intersection
in South Williamsburg.
"Why?" I ask.
"I want you to close a freezer door," he says.
        "It's ringing and won't stop."
"Why can't you shut it off?"
"It's the Sabbath."

I follow him around the corner
to his apartment building.
"You know," I say, "if I were you,
        I'd just close the freezer door. No one will see."
"God will see."
I take the elevator while he takes the stairs.

I walk into his apartment, past three children
playing a game on the floor in a clean, bare room.
The freezer door is open an inch; I push it shut.
"Do you want any food?" he asks. "Any water?"
"No thanks," I say. "I have water."
I walk out, get on my bike and ride toward the bridge.

WHO'S THAT RINGING?

I hear the doorbell ring
and see myself get up.
Someone is pounding on the outside.
I look through the peephole
and see a girl's eye,
but I know it's the eye
of my brother, who is not alive.
He wants to get in,
but I don't want to let him in.
If he enters our place,
something bad will happen.

He is insistent with his banging.
I hope the metal is strong enough
to keep him out.

DOCTOR COPPER

I know my mother is feeling a little better
when she calls her physician Dr. Copper
while his real name is Dr. Coppes.
Maybe she thinks he is more of a law officer
than a doctor, or maybe she is delirious.
But she says the wrong name clearly,
and I want to know this Dr. Copper,
this doctor who is also a police officer.
I want to talk to him
and ask how my mother is doing, healthwise,
because he, if anyone, would have the evidence.

BEEF BRISKET

I tell my mother
my wife made a beef brisket for Passover,
but my mother can't hear what I'm saying.
"East birthday?" she asks.
"No," I say. "Beef brisket."
"Spell it. Does it start with an E?"
"No. It starts with a B. It's a food."
"Beast birthday? Is it an animal?"
"Yes. Beef."
"Beast?"
"No."
"I can't hear you. All I can hear are birds chirping."
"Where are you?"
"On a bench outside. Can you hear the birds?"
"No," I say.
"My hearing aid is turned all the way up:
       All I can hear are the birds."

VISITING HOURS

My mother says she was falling asleep
and dreaming that my sister was sitting beside her.
The two of them were watching television:
old movies, three in a row.
This was what they liked to do
when they were together.

Earlier, when my mother was in the hospital,
she saw a high-school classmate in her room.
She asked a nurse if she could also see this person
(the classmate and the nurse were in the room
at the same time).
But the nurse said no, she couldn't see anyone
other than my mother there.
Still, my mother knew the person she saw:
He was an old friend from China,
but he hadn't aged at all.

HEIGHTENED SENSES

Is it possible to be more fully alive?
Not simply alive, but alive to a greater degree?
I had thought it was an either/or situation.
Either you were alive, or you were not.
If I were more alive, my heart might beat faster,
I might breathe more deeply.
I might walk farther, run faster.
All of my senses would be heightened.
I would appreciate the flavor of food,
the brush of skin against skin.
I would have an increased sense of touch.
I would feel things better with my fingers.

ALWAYS IS NOT FOREVER

Always is definitely not forever.
It may be all the time, yes,
but we can put a stop to it,
especially if it involves an annoying sound,
like that of a pneumatic drill,
outside our window.

We can make sure that the constant thing—
which may not be a literal jackhammer
but could resemble a jackhammer—
goes away, or at least is silenced.
Yes, we don't want things
that are constantly irritating
to last forever.

On the other hand,
we do want pleasant things
to last a long time, if not forever.
Surely we can identify
some pleasant things, some healthy things,
some things that are beneficial.
We want these quiet, harmonious things
to last as long as possible.

LET IT SHINE

In my dream, clouds roll away
after lingering for days,
and the sun comes out suddenly,
bathing people, buildings, and a few trees
in bright, total light.

When I wake, I see the clouds
have not rolled away.
They are low and thick,
dimming everything along the street:
the people, the traffic, the few trees.

After a while, on the same day,
the sun comes out.
All I had to do was wait.
The sun is really shining.
This is no dream.

Acknowledgments

I would like to thank Randi Hoffman, Thomas Fucaloro, David Lawton, Jane Ormerod, and Mary McLaughlin Slechta for their editorial comments.

My appreciation also to the editors of the following publications where these poems first appeared, some in earlier forms:

And Then	Waxed-Paper Museum
Brownstone Poets 2019 Anthology	Lights in Darkness
The Café Review	Foreign Fillings
	God Will See
	Reading in Bed
Chrysanthemum Press Anthology	Glass and Tears
Drunken Careening Writers	Turtle's Cold Day
Home Planet News Online	Farmers and Dove
	Owning My Speech
	Seal Sounds
Nomad's Choir	Always Is Not Forever
	The Fear, Revisited
North of Oxford	Where I'm From
	In the Buddha's Tooth Temple
Paterson Literary Review	Beef Brisket
Public Illumination Magazine	Another Flat
	Down in the Dumpster
Sensitive Skin	Cold Days in Florida
	Steamrolled

About the Author

Thaddeus Rutkowski is the author of six previous books, including the poetry collection *Border Crossings*. His novel *Haywire* won the Asian American Writers' Workshop's Members' Choice Award, and his creative memoir *Guess and Check* received the Electronic Literature bronze award for multicultural fiction. His writing has appeared in the *New York Times*, *International Herald Tribune*, and *The Outlaw Bible of American Poetry*, as well as in *Copper Nickel*, *Hayden's Ferry Review*, *Faultline*, *Fiction*, *Fiction International*, *Pleaides*, *Potomac Review*, *Sou'wester*, and many other magazines.

A graduate of Cornell University and Johns Hopkins University, Rutkowski received a fiction writing fellowship from the New York Foundation for the Arts and was a resident writer at Yaddo, MacDowell, and other colonies. Traveling extensively, he has been a featured reader in Budapest, Dublin, London, Paris, Singapore, and Hong Kong, and was selected to read in the former compound of East German President Erich Honecker in Berlin.

Rutkowski teaches at Medgar Evers College and the Writer's Voice of the West Side YMCA and lives with his wife, Randi Hoffman, in Manhattan.

About great weather for MEDIA

Founded in January 2012, great weather for MEDIA focuses on the unpredictable, the fearless, the bright, the dark, and the innovative...

We are based in New York City and showcase both national and international writers. As well as publishing the highest quality poetry and prose, we organize numerous readings, performances, music and art events in New York City, across the United States, and beyond.

Be sure to visit our website for details of upcoming publications, events, our weekly open mic, and how to submit work to great weather for MEDIA's yearly anthology.

Website: www.greatweatherformedia.com

Email: editors@greatweatherformedia.com

Twitter: @greatweatherfor

Facebook: www.facebook.com/great.weather

great weather for MEDIA Books

Poetry Collections

Tricks of Light - Thaddeus Rutkowski

something sweet & filled with blood - melissa christine goodrum

Where Night and Day Become One - Steve Dalachinsky

Surge - Michelle Whittaker

Crown Prince of Rabbits - John Paul Davis

Exercises in High Treason - John J. Trause

Harvest the Dirt - Wil Gibson

Debridement - Corrina Bain

meant to wake up feeling - Aimee Herman

Retrograde - Puma Perl

Anthologies

Birds Fall Silent in the Mechanical Sea

Suitcase of Chrysanthemums

The Other Side of Violet

The Careless Embrace of the Boneshaker

Before Passing

I Let Go of the Stars in My Hand

The Understanding between Foxes and Light

It's Animal but Merciful

9 780998 144078